Technology All Around Us

Space Exploration

Clive Gifford

A⁺
Smart Apple Media

First published in 2005 by Franklin Watts
96 Leonard Street, London EC2A 4XD

Franklin Watts Australia
Level 17/207 Kent Street, Sydney NSW 2000

Produced by Arcturus Publishing Ltd.
26/27 Bickels Yard, 151–153 Bermondsey Street, London SE1 3HA

Series concept: Alex Woolf, Editor: Alex Woolf, Designer: Tim
Mayer, Picture researcher: Glass Onion Pictures

Picture Credits
Science Photo Library: 4 (NASA), 5 (NASA), 6 (NASA), 7 (NASA),
8 (NASA), 9 (Volker Steger), 10 (NASA), cover and 11 (Mike Agliolo), 12
(NASA), 13 (NASA), 14 (NASA), 15 (David A. Hardy, Futures: 50 Years in
Space), 16 (NASA), 17 (Novosti), 18 (David Ducros), 19 (David A. Hardy),
20 (NASA), 21 (NASA), 22
(European Space Agency), 23 (Johns Hopkins University Applied Physics
Laboratory), 24 (David Parker), 25 (David Nunuk), 26 (NASA), 27 (Space
Telescope Science Institute / NASA), 28
(Detlev van Ravenswaay), 29 (Victor Habbick Visions).

Published in the United States by Smart Apple Media
2140 Howard Drive West, North Mankato, Minnesota 56003

Library of Congress Cataloging-in-Publication Data

Gifford, Clive.
Space exploration / by Clive Gifford.
p. cm. — (Technology all around us)
Includes index.
ISBN 1-58340-753-7
1. Astronautics—Juvenile literature. 2. Outer space—Exploration—Juvenile
literature. I. Title. II. Series.

TL793.G463 2005
629.4—dc22   2005040511

9 8 7 6 5 4 3 2 1

Contents

Sending people or machines to explore space requires huge amounts of power. This power is needed to break free of the strong pull of Earth's gravity. Rockets are the machines for the job.

Technology in Action

Saturn V

It is November 9, 1967. The world's largest, most powerful rocket launches successfully for the first time. The *Saturn V*'s engines fire, producing more thrust than 48 Concorde supersonic airliners.

At more than 360 feet (110 m) in height, it is taller than a 30-story building and weighs 6.6 million pounds (3 million kg). The *Saturn V* is made up of three stages. After the engines of each stage use up their fuel, they separate from the rocket and fall away.

Two years later, another Saturn rocket launches the first Apollo mission to land a man on the moon.

The launch of *Apollo 11* from Kennedy Space Center, Florida, on July 16, 1969—the beginning of the first manned mission to land on the moon.

How Rockets Work

Rockets burn fuels stored inside their body and direct the huge amounts of thrust down at the ground. This thrust forces the rocket away from its launch pad, up through Earth's atmosphere, and into space.

Rockets travel outside Earth's atmosphere, where there is no oxygen to make fuel burn. So they carry their own supply of oxygen or a chemical containing oxygen, called an oxidizer. Pumps mix the oxygen supply with fuel before it is burned, forcing the hot gases out of the rocket's nozzles.

Increasing Power

A rocket's payload is the important object, such as a space station or a satellite, being carried into space. The first successful payload was the *Sputnik 1* satellite, launched by the USSR in 1957. It was a steel ball containing a radio transmitter and weighed 184.3 pounds (83.6 kg).

As rockets increased in power, larger and larger payloads could be carried. The *Saturn V* rocket could carry payloads as heavy as 260,100 pounds (118,000 kg).

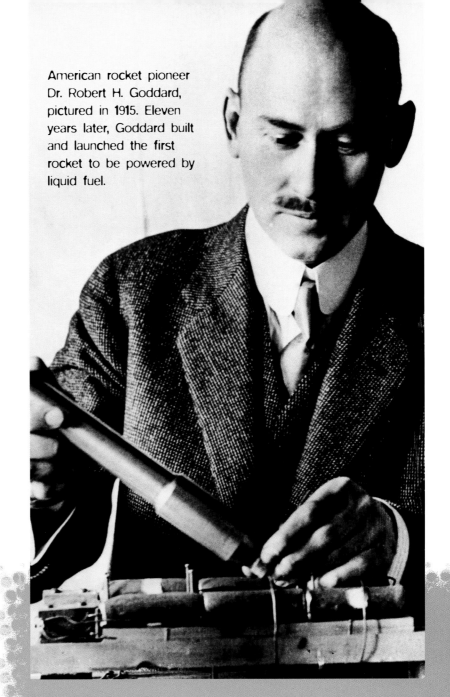

American rocket pioneer Dr. Robert H. Goddard, pictured in 1915. Eleven years later, Goddard built and launched the first rocket to be powered by liquid fuel.

Looking Back

Early Rockets

Small rockets using gunpowder were first developed by the Chinese more than 750 years ago.

Space rockets were developed from rocket-powered missiles first used by German forces in World War II and then developed by the United States and the USSR. The first missions into space were launched by rockets that were converted missiles.

Rockets are single-use machines that launch their payload before burning up or becoming space junk. The space shuttle is the world's only reusable space vehicle. Built by NASA, the shuttle takes off like a rocket but lands like an aircraft on its return to Earth.

The first shuttle made its debut spaceflight in 1981. Since then, more than 110 missions have been made by 6 different craft.

Looking Forward

Safer and Cheaper

Shuttle missions have twice ended in disaster, in 1986 and 2003, with the death of all astronauts on board. Safer and cheaper successors to the space shuttle are being planned for future flights.

The *Challenger* space shuttle sits on top of a Boeing 747 jet. The shuttle is being transported from California to the Kennedy Space Center in Florida.

The shuttle requires 55 to 100 days to prepare for a mission. Future craft, such as orbital space planes launched from the top of a regular rocket, may take less than a month to prepare.

Takeoff and Touchdown

As the space shuttle takes off, it is powered by two rocket boosters that are used up in just two minutes and then discarded. For the next seven minutes, the shuttle draws fuel from a giant fuel tank, using 1,067 gallons (4,037 l) every second. Boosted high above Earth, the shuttle ejects the fuel tank and settles into its orbit around Earth.

Working on the Shuttle

Circling Earth once every 92 minutes, a space shuttle mission usually lasts 7 or 8 days. The crew of up to seven astronauts carries out experiments inside the craft, and members sometimes take spacewalks.

The shuttle's cargo bay is large enough to hold a bus and is used to launch satellites, probes, and other hardware into space.

Hubble Trouble

It is 1993, and the fate of a billion-dollar space telescope hangs in the balance. The Hubble Space Telescope (see pages 26–27) is not working properly, and a shuttle repair mission has been launched.

Millions of people watch the mission on TV as the shuttle crew works around the clock 370 miles (600 km) above Earth. More than 35 hours of dangerous spacewalks outside the shuttle are needed for repairs. The mission is an outstanding success, and the Hubble continues to work well to this day.

A view of the space shuttle *Atlantis*'s cargo bay. On this mission, the on-board observatory was used to study the effect of solar radiation on Earth's atmosphere.

In 1961, Russian cosmonaut Yuri Gagarin became the first human in space in a mission lasting just 1 hour and 48 minutes. Since that time, more than 450 people have entered space. Nearly all space missions have been in craft orbiting Earth.

Heavy Workload

Yuri Gagarin was little more than a passenger on his first mission into space. He had little control over the space shuttle as he hurtled around Earth.

On modern missions, astronauts have much more work to do. Instruments that study space have to be operated, experiments must be performed inside and outside the craft, and repairs sometimes need to be made.

Some spacecraft, such as the shuttle, carry equipment in their cargo bays that must be launched into space. On the shuttle, astronauts work with a robot arm that is more than 50 feet (15 m) long. The arm can also help capture space hardware, such as satellites that are already in orbit, so that astronauts can repair or upgrade them.

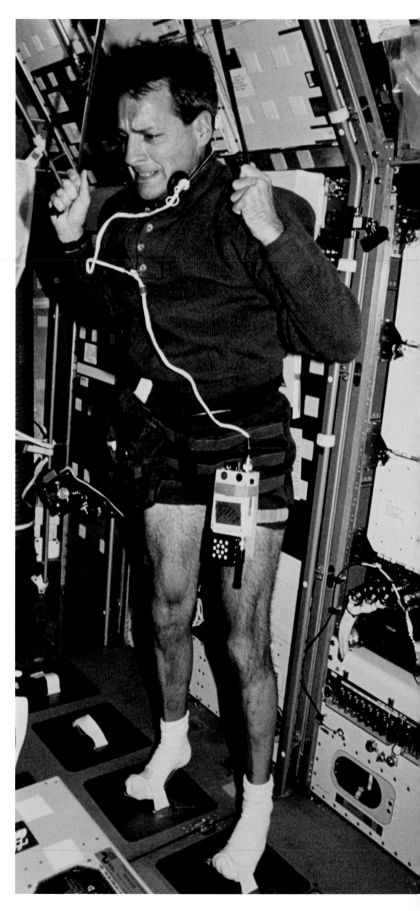

A NASA astronaut exercises on board the space shuttle *Columbia*. With his feet held in place by toe loops, he pulls down on straps to work his arm muscles.

Daily Chores

Crews in space experience microgravity, which causes them to float around the spacecraft unless they are strapped in place. Restraints such as belts and Velcro fastenings keep objects and people in place. Daily cleaning prevents floating crumbs, dust, and other debris from damaging the spacecraft's systems.

Weightlessness means that a person's muscles don't work as hard as they do on Earth. Over long space missions, muscles can waste away unless crew members perform regular exercises.

Right: This spinning platform is used to simulate the feeling of weightlessness astronauts experience in space.

Looking Back

Space Snacks

The first food in space was healthy but not very tasty. It was made up of dried meat or vegetable cubes and liquid mush squeezed out of aluminum tubes. On the 1965 *Gemini* mission, American astronaut John Young smuggled a corn beef sandwich on board and received a reprimand as a result. Now, astronauts on space shuttles choose from around 100 different foods and drinks during their mission.

Looking Forward

Vacations In Space

In 2001, U.S. businessman Dennis Tito became the first space tourist. He paid $20 million for a trip on a Russian Soyuz vehicle that docked with the International Space Station.

Tito (along with several other companies) is working on plans to build a hotel in space, in orbit around Earth. Wealthy visitors would pay to fly by reusable space vehicle to the space hotel, which would offer spectacular views of Earth.

Spacewalk Systems

Inside spacecraft, astronauts are safe and secure. Outside, in space, they need to be protected by advanced spacesuits when they perform Extra Vehicular Activity (EVA), or spacewalks.

A Hostile Place

Space is a dangerous place for humans. There is no oxygen to breathe, and there is harmful radiation. Also, tiny dust particles called micrometeoroids can rip through regular clothing and flesh.

Above the protection of Earth's atmosphere, temperatures can soar to 252 °F (122 °C) in the sun's glare, and can drop to -292 °F (-180 °C) in the shadows.

The outer layers of EVA suits repel space dust, while inner layers are liquid-cooled and contain heating systems to keep an astronaut comfortable.

EMU Suit

Extravehicular Mobility Unit (EMU) suits are worn on space shuttle spacewalks. Made up of more than a dozen different layers, they take 45 minutes to put on.

First Spacewalk

In 1965, Russian cosmonaut Alexei Leonov became the first person to spacewalk. Disaster nearly struck when Leonov's spacesuit inflated and became too rigid for him to move. He had to release air pressure inside the suit and cram himself inside the inflatable airlock to survive.

Technology has improved greatly since Leonov's 10-minute spacewalk. In 2001, NASA astronauts Susan Helms and Jim Voss made a record spacewalk of 8 hours, 56 minutes.

An astronaut being fitted into an EVA suit as part of his training. He will then be lowered into a deep pool of water to help simulate the weightless conditions of a real space mission.

EMU suits contain a main and emergency oxygen supply, which is controlled by a large backpack called the Primary Life Support System (PLSS). The PLSS also controls the temperature inside the suit and absorbs waste gases. Wearing an EMU suit, an astronaut can stay in space for seven or more hours.

Ready to Spacewalk

Suited up, astronauts go into a compartment called an airlock. They must wait here for an hour or longer before they head out into space. This is to get their bodies used to the lower air pressure inside their suits.

Technology in Action

Untethered

It is 1984, and Bruce McCandless II becomes the first astronaut to make an EVA without a safety tether. He straps on a Manned Maneuvering Unit (MMU), an advanced form of rocket pack that features 24 small thrusters.

For 90 incredible minutes, McCandless uses the joystick controllers on the arms of the MMU to travel through space, always keeping within 330 feet (100 m) of the shuttle.

Astronaut Bruce McCandless floats freely above Earth in his MMU.

Space Stations

Most manned spacecraft spend just a few days in space. Space stations, however, can spend months or even years orbiting Earth.

These large structures give astronauts the chance to perform lengthy experiments. They also allow scientists to study the effects of living in space for long periods.

Russian cosmonaut Valeriy Polyakov stares out of the round window (center) of the *Mir* space station. Polyakov's mission on board the space station in 1995–96 lasted 438 days.

Looking Back

Piece By Piece

The first space stations—the 39-foot-long (12 m) *Salyut 1* (1971) and the 82-foot-long (25 m) *Skylab* (1973)—were built in one piece.

Since then, space stations have grown in size and have to be transported into space in separate pieces. It is expected to take 45 missions and around 1,700 hours of spacewalks to complete the 290-foot-long (88 m) International Space Station (ISS).

Record-Breaking Mir

The first space station, *Salyut 1*, lasted less than a year in space and was lived in by a Russian cosmonaut for just 23 days. The *Mir* space station stayed in space for 15 years, and one crew member occupied the station for a record 438 days in a row.

A total of 100 people lived and worked on *Mir* between 1986 and 1999. *Mir* was made up of six separate modules, including an observatory and a greenhouse. During *Mir's* lifetime, more than 16,000 experiments were carried out on board the station.

Tricky Maneuver

It is October 14, 2000, and 225 miles (360 km) above Earth, a crucial piece of construction is being carried out. A new docking port has to be put in place on the ISS—a tricky task.

A Japanese astronaut controls a robot arm to move the 2.2-ton (2 t) port carefully past fragile solar panels with inches to spare. The delicate operation is a success. With the port in position, space shuttles can now dock and connect with the space station.

The International Space Station orbits 225 miles (360 km) above Earth's surface. Giant solar panels (top) power all of its systems.

The International Space Station

The work of 16 nations, the International Space Station (ISS) is the biggest structure put into space. When completed in 2006, it will weigh 496 tons (450 t) and include 6 scientific laboratories.

It will be powered by its 354-foot-wide (108 m) sets of solar panels. Astronauts have been living and working on the station since 2000. More than 50,000 objects, from food canisters to tools and spare parts, will be found on the ISS. Each object is tagged with a tiny, solar-powered transmitter.

13

Astronaut John Young leaps up from the moon's surface after the *Apollo 16* lunar module's safe landing in April 1972. Young and fellow astronaut Charles Duke spent more than 20 hours on the lunar surface.

The moon is our nearest neighbor in space. On average, it lies 238,870 miles (384,400 km) away. The 1960s saw a race between the USSR and the U.S. to be the first to put a person on the moon.

The *Eagle* Has Landed

On July 20, 1969, Neil Armstrong and Buzz Aldrin stepped out of their lunar module, named *Eagle*, and became the first men on the moon. During their 22 hours there, they collected 46 pounds (21 kg) of moon samples before blasting off.

Their lunar module re-docked with the command module, which had been orbiting the moon. As the craft approached Earth, the top part of the module separated and entered Earth's atmosphere. It splashed down safely in the Pacific Ocean.

Looking Back

Crash Landings

Many of the earliest unmanned moon missions were designed to crash into the moon, taking and sending back photographs before they were destroyed. In 1964, the American probe *Ranger 7* took 4,308 photos before hitting the moon. The previous 6 probes had all failed.

Between 1959 and 1976, there were 31 American and 48 Russian unmanned missions to the moon. Around half of these missions failed.

An artist's impression of the European Space Agency's *SMART-1* spacecraft approaching the moon. Launched in 2003, the probe is designed to observe and measure features of the moon while staying in orbit.

Looking Forward

Return to the Moon

A permanent base on the moon could test equipment and techniques that might be used to send people to Mars. A moon base might lie mainly underground to provide some warmth and a regular temperature.

Minerals from the moon's surface could be mined and processed to create oxygen and useful materials. Plants could be grown in heated, inflatable greenhouses.

Search For Water

Just 12 people, in 6 Apollo missions, have set foot on the moon. The last was Captain Eugene Cernan in 1972. But other missions to the moon have taken place since. During the 1990s, two NASA probes, *Clementine* and *Prospector*, orbited the moon. The probes discovered evidence that ice may be found in craters near the moon's poles.

Near Disaster

The 1970 *Apollo 13* mission was more than halfway to the moon when an explosion damaged the craft's oxygen tanks and destroyed many of the ship's systems. Amazingly, the crew and ground staff were able to bring the spacecraft safely home.

Planetary Probes

Space probes are unmanned machines that explore parts of space and send information back to Earth using radio signals. Many of these probes have been sent to other planets in the solar system.

Looking Back

«

Photos Of Mars

The first successful mission to Mars was carried out by the U.S. probe *Mariner 4*. In 1965, it flew past Mars at a distance of 6,090 miles (9,800 km) and took 22 pictures. These were stored on a cassette tape and transmitted slowly back to Earth.

In 1996, the *Mars Global Surveyor* was launched. This probe stopped within 250 miles (400 km) of the planet's surface. In 2001, the *Mars Global Surveyor* took its 100,000th image of the planet's surface.

An image of Mars taken by the *Mars Global Surveyor*. The white, wispy clouds above the surface are believed to be made up largely of ice.

Better than Humans

The eight other planets in our solar system are millions of miles away from Earth. It takes many years for a machine to reach them, and there are dangers on the way.

Unmanned space probes can be built and sent on one-way missions with no hope of return. They can also be built far smaller and cheaper than manned craft, without living quarters and the air, food, and water supplies needed by astronauts.

Missions to Venus

Probes can survive hostile conditions on other planets. On Venus, for example, the surface temperature averages 860 °F (460 °C). The Russian *Venera 4* probe was the first to reach Venus's atmosphere, where it was crushed by the planet's atmospheric pressure, which is 90 times stronger than Earth's.

Eight tougher Venera probes were more successful and explored the atmosphere and surface of Venus. Landing in 1982, *Venera 13* and *Venera 14* both used a series of drills to probe into the crust of Venus.

 Looking Forward

Return Trips

Almost all probes to the planets travel one-way missions, never to return. Future probes, however, are being designed to travel back to Earth carrying crucial samples of gases, dust, soil, and rocks from other planets and moons in space.

A Mars Sample Return mission may launch in 2014. Russia is planning to send a probe to collect soil from Phobos, one of Mars's two moons, by 2007.

A model of the *Venera 9* space probe, which entered the atmosphere of Venus in October 1975. The probe's lander successfully touched down on the planet's surface and sent back images and measurements.

Long-Distance Travelers

A handful of space probes have traveled to the farthest parts of the solar system. These probes have greatly increased our knowledge of distant planets such as Jupiter, Saturn, Uranus, and Neptune.

Far, Far Away

The longest-distance probe is *Voyager 1*. It is now around 8.4 billion miles (13.5 billion km) away from Earth. Weighing more than a ton (1 t), the probe contains 65,000 working parts. It was launched in 1977, but energy from its nuclear power generator will keep it working until around 2020.

Voyager 2

Voyager 2 is the only probe to have reached and investigated Neptune and Uranus. *Voyager 2* discovered rings around Uranus similar to those around Saturn. Together, the 2 Voyager probes discovered 21 new moons orbiting the planets.

Artwork of the *Cassini-Huygens* probe approaching Titan, one of Saturn's moons. The probe will orbit Saturn for four years, sending back data about the planet, its rings, and its moons.

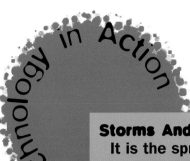

Storms And Volcanoes

It is the spring of 1979, and *Voyager 1* is traveling close to the solar system's largest planet, Jupiter. It returns 17,477 images of Jupiter and lots of other data from its 11 scientific instruments.

Back on Earth, scientists are excited by the discoveries. They learn that the Great Red Spot on the planet's surface is a huge hurricane storm, twice the size of Earth. They also find active volcanoes on Io, one of Jupiter's moons.

This image shows the gravity assist technique used by *Voyager 2*. The spacecraft flew around part of Jupiter to speed it up on its way toward Saturn.

Gravity Assist

To travel great distances using less fuel, many long-distance probes use a technique called gravity assist. The probe flies around a planet and uses the pull of the planet's gravity to increase the spacecraft's speed.

The first spacecraft to use gravity assist was *Pioneer 10*. It flew to Jupiter at a speed of 6.1 miles (9.8 km) per second, or 21,922 miles (35,280 km) per hour. After flying around part of Jupiter, the effect of the gravity assist more than doubled *Pioneer 10*'s speed to 13.9 miles (22.4 km) per second, or 50,107 miles (80,640 km) per hour.

Looking Forward

Probe to Pluto

Pluto, the farthest planet from Earth, is the only planet not to have been investigated by a space probe. That may change with the future launch of the *New Horizons* probe, which could occur as early as 2006. Taking more than nine years to reach its target, the probe would investigate both Pluto and its mysterious moon, Charon.

Surface Rovers

Moving around the surface of the moon or other planets is a technological challenge. Yet a handful of rovers sent to the moon and Mars have been highly successful.

Astronaut Eugene Cernan on board the Lunar Roving Vehicle during the last manned mission to the moon in December 1972.

Moon Buggy

Astronauts on the *Apollo 15, 16,* and *17* missions rode around the moon's surface in a four-wheel-drive buggy called a Lunar Roving Vehicle (LRV). Two electric batteries powered the LRV to a top speed of 11.6 miles (18.6 km) per hour. It could carry 2 astronauts, tools, and rock samples and was fitted with a camera and radio antenna.

The First Rover On Mars

NASA's *Pathfinder* probe landed on Mars in 1997 and opened its body like the petals of a flower. Out rolled *Sojourner,* a small, six-wheeled roving robot. *Sojourner* was just 25 inches (63 cm) long and weighed only 23 pounds (10.5 kg), but it was very tough.

It carried several cameras and a large range of instruments with which it examined rocks and soils on Mars.

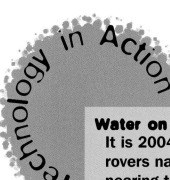

Water on Mars?

It is 2004 on Mars, and a pair of NASA rovers named *Spirit* and *Opportunity* are nearing the end of their 90-day main mission. *Spirit* approaches a four-inch-high (10 cm) rock, code-named Mazatzal, and begins to investigate it.

The robot uses a number of tools, including a RAT (rock abrasion tool), which grinds away the outer surface so that tests can be made on the clean rock underneath. Results suggest that there may have been water in the rock during its formation.

The Mars Exploration Rover, which roamed the planet's surface in 2004. The rover's mast contains cameras that give views of the Martian surface.

Looking Back

Lunakhod

In 1970, the Russian Luna 17 mission landed on the moon, lowered a ramp, and released a bathtub-shaped rover called *Lunakhod*. Weighing 1,667 pounds (756 kg), the rover took 321 Earth days to cover just 6.5 miles (10.5 km) of the moon. The rover was remote controlled from Earth by five human technicians.

In 2004, the *Spirit* and *Opportunity* rovers, which weighed less than a quarter of *Lunakhod*, traveled around Mars. These advanced robots made many of their own navigation decisions.

Future Rovers

Designs for more than a dozen rovers are being tested on Earth. One unusual design is called the Tumbleweed Rover. It is a 6.6-foot-wide (2 m), beachball-shaped machine that would roll over rocks and other obstacles in its path.

21

Comet and Asteroid Explorers

There are other bodies in our solar system besides the sun, the planets, and the moon. Some amazing pieces of space technology have enabled scientists to learn more about these bodies.

Comets

A comet is like a huge, dirty snowball with a small, rocky core, in orbit around the sun. Scientists are fascinated by comets, and a number of probes have been sent to observe them up close. In 2004, the *Stardust* probe flew to within 150 miles (240 km) of Comet Wild 2, the closest any machine has flown to a comet.

Halley's Fleet

The most famous comet is Halley's Comet, which orbits the sun once every 76 years. In 1986, the comet was examined by two Russian Vega probes, two Japanese probes, and the European Space Agency's *Giotto* probe. These machines became known as Halley's fleet.

The nucleus of Halley's Comet, photographed by the *Giotto* space probe in 1986. *Giotto* came to within 373 miles (600 km) of the comet's nucleus.

>> Looking Forward

Riding the Comet

March 2004 saw the launch of an ambitious comet chaser and lander built by the European Space Agency. The *Rosetta* probe is heading for Comet 67P Churyumov-Gerasimenko, 4.3 billion miles (7 billion km) away, and will reach it in 2014.

Once in orbit around the comet, *Rosetta* will drop the *Philae* probe onto the comet's surface. The washing machine-sized lander will dig in spikes and then ride piggyback as it sends back information.

Asteroids

Asteroids are chunks of rock mainly found in a belt 186 million miles (300 million km) wide, between Mars and Jupiter. Scientists believe they may be the remains of a planet that broke up.

Launched in 2003, the Japanese *MUSES-C* probe is designed to briefly land three times on an asteroid to collect samples. The probe is expected to return to Earth in 2007.

Technology in Action

Asteroid Lander

It is February 14, 2001, and the *NEAR Shoemaker* probe has been circling a large space rock called Asteroid 433 Eros for almost a year. The probe has already taken more than 150,000 photos. Now it is being asked to perform a mission it was not designed for.

The *NEAR* probe descends to the asteroid's surface, taking 69 close-up pictures. It becomes the first machine to land on an asteroid. Amazingly, *NEAR* survives the landing to continue sending data back to Earth.

The *Near Earth Asteroid Rendezvous* (*NEAR*) space probe orbits Asteroid 433 Eros. The probe performed a 10-month survey of the asteroid, using a large variety of cameras and scientific instruments.

23

Telescopes have allowed people to peer into space and see many objects that are invisible to the naked eye.

Optical telescopes are used to collect and magnify light that can be seen by the human eye. Other types of telescopes are used to collect radio waves, infrared and ultraviolet light, and X rays from space.

Refracting and Reflecting Telescopes

There are two types of optical telescopes. Refracting telescopes use glass lenses to magnify objects. Reflecting telescopes use large, smooth mirrors to collect light.

Telescopes are often measured by the size of the opening that receives light. The human eye has a 0.3-inch (7 mm) opening. Telescopes can have openings measuring three feet (1 m) or more.

An astronomer uses a 30-inch (76 cm) reflecting telescope at the Leuschner Observatory near San Francisco.

Technology in Action

Collision Course

It is January 2001, and scientists are looking at signals collected by the Arecibo radio telescope in Puerto Rico.

The telescope spots and tracks an asteroid labeled 1950DA. This causes excitement, as this asteroid was discovered 50 years ago but has since been lost. Scientists calculate that the asteroid will pass close to—or possibly crash into—Earth in the year 2880.

The VLT

Large telescopes are often placed in a building called an observatory with computers and other space instruments. The European Southern Observatory in Chile will soon house the Very Large Telescope (VLT). It is made up of four powerful telescopes linked together. It will have the power to spot a small insect 6,215 miles (10,000 km) away.

Radio Telescopes

Stars and other bodies in space give off radio waves. A radio telescope uses a large, bowl-shaped reflector dish to collect these waves. The signals are then often sent to computers to be processed and turned into images. Radio telescopes are often linked to work together in what is called an array.

Looking Back

Planet Finder

In 1781, renowned British telescope-maker William Herschel was scanning the skies with one of his telescopes when he spotted an unusual object. For weeks, he believed it was a comet before realizing it was a planet. Herschel had discovered Uranus. He had used a seven-inch (17.8 cm) reflecting telescope to make his discovery.

Astronomers today use much larger and more powerful telescopes. The Keck 1 reflecting telescope, situated in Hawaii, measures 32.2 feet (9.8 m).

A series of the dish antennae that make up the world's largest radio telescope, the Very Large Array (VLA), in New Mexico. The VLA consists of 27 dishes, each 82 feet (25 m) in diameter.

On Earth, telescopes have to peer through the atmosphere. In space, clearer views and signals can be received. Telescopes have been sent into space, orbiting Earth or traveling close to the sun.

The Hubble Space Telescope is lifted out of the space shuttle's cargo bay by its robot arm after a servicing mission in 1997.

The Hubble Space Telescope

The most famous orbiting observatory is the Hubble Space Telescope. Work on the Hubble began 14 years before it was launched into space in 1990. The Hubble features an 8.2-foot (2.5 m) reflecting telescope and instruments that collect and measure infrared and ultraviolet waves that come from distant stars and galaxies.

Looking Forward

The Hunt for New Planets

The search will soon begin for planets in other galaxies that might be capable of supporting life. NASA is planning to launch a new observatory, Terrestrial Planet Finder (TPF), between 2012 and 2015.

Featuring telescopes 100 times as powerful as the Hubble, the observatory will seek out suitable planets and use instruments to measure their temperatures and identify the gases found in their atmospheres.

An image from the Hubble Space Telescope of the spectacular Eagle Nebula. The "towers" of gas are more than 560 million miles (900 million km) high.

The Eagle Nebula

It is 1995, and 375 miles (600 km) above Earth, the Hubble Space Telescope is capturing some of the most dramatic images of space ever seen. The telescope trains its instruments on a site 7,000 light-years away—that is 450 million times the distance between Earth and the sun.

The Hubble photographs the Eagle Nebula—gigantic clouds of gas billions of miles in size. Viewing the images on Earth, scientists are stunned by the sight of new stars being born in the Eagle Nebula.

The Hubble has sent back enough images and measurements to fill a personal computer every day for 10 years. It has made 350,000 observations of stars and galaxies billions of miles away.

Observing the Sun

Launched in 1995, SOHO is an observatory that studies the sun. Its instruments include a telescope that collects ultraviolet waves. Scientists use the data from SOHO to help them learn how the sun and events in space affect Earth's weather.

SOHO was meant to operate until 1998, but it was so successful that the European Space Agency and NASA decided to keep it running until 2007.

27

Technology has only explored a tiny part of space, yet the achievements in less than 50 years are impressive. The future is likely to see many more breakthroughs in technology and knowledge about space.

Technology in Action

Joint Robotic Workforce

It is 2003, and important robots are being tested in the U.S. A pair of NASA robots, called the Joint Robotic Workforce, practice moving steel girders and other building materials. A Frogbot practices leaping over large boulders. Small, mobile robots move in swarms, searching for objects and performing group tasks.

The successors to these test robots may play a part in building a future Mars base before human visitors from Earth arrive.

Living On Mars

Sending people to explore Mars may occur later this century. It would be a huge operation involving many missions to send supplies, building materials, and robots to the planet in advance of astronauts.

A future base on Mars might be built out of parts made on Earth and transported to the planet in a series of space freighters. They would be put together with the aid of robots.

The astronauts would enter a set of buildings closed off from the hostile conditions on Mars. Such a place would need huge amounts of electricity supplied by nuclear power or giant arrays of solar panels.

Starships

To travel to the edge of the solar system takes many years. To travel to another solar system would take centuries unless new, faster ways of traveling through space can be found. Scientists will investigate lasers and other forms of energy in the future in order to build faster-traveling machines.

The Search for Intelligent Life

Is there intelligent life on other planets in the universe? No one knows, but the future will see more efforts to search and make contact. The Search for Extraterrestrial Intelligence (SETI) looks for radio signals reaching Earth that may have been sent by alien life. One day, contact may even be made.

In the future, spaceships might be able to grow their own food and supply their own water and air. All waste would be recycled. Such spacecraft could travel huge distances for many years.

Looking Forward

Terraforming

Terraforming is the changing of a planet's environment so that it is sufficiently like Earth to allow people, plants, and animals to live there. It is perhaps the most ambitious of all space projects and would take thousands of years. To terraform a planet such as Mars requires a large water supply. It also needs gases generated to form an Earth-like atmosphere to trap heat and warm the planet's surface.

Timeline

1957 The Soviet Union's *Sputnik 1* becomes the first satellite to be launched into space.

1958 The National Aeronautics and Space Administration (NASA) is founded.

1959 The Soviet Union's *Luna 1* satellite becomes the first to orbit the sun.

1961 Soviet cosmonaut Yuri Gagarin becomes the first person to be launched into space.

1965 The first EVA, or spacewalk, is performed by Soviet cosmonaut Alexei Leonov.

1966 Space probes from both the Soviet Union (*Luna 9*) and the U.S. (*Surveyor 1*) are the first machines to land on the moon.

1969 *Apollo 11* lands on the moon, and NASA astronauts Neil Armstrong and Buzz Aldrin become the first people to walk on the moon.

1971 The first orbiting space station, the Soviet Union's *Salyut 1*, is launched.

1974 The U.S. and Soviet Union cooperate on the Apollo-Soyuz test project, during which American and Soviet spacecraft dock in orbit.

1976 *Viking 1* and *Viking 2* become the first space lander probes to send images back from the surface of Mars.

1979 The *Voyager 1* and *2* probes reach Jupiter.

1981 The first space shuttle, *Columbia*, is successfully launched into space.

1984 The first untethered spacewalk is carried out by Bruce McCandless using a Manned Maneuvering Unit (MMU).

1986 The space shuttle *Challenger* explodes, killing all seven astronauts on board.

1986 The first sections of the *Mir* space station are launched by the Soviet Union.

1990 The Hubble Space Telescope is launched.

1995 The European Space Agency's SOHO solar observatory is launched.

1996 A probe from the *Galileo* spacecraft examines Io, one of Jupiter's moons.

1998 Construction begins on the International Space Station, the largest human-made structure ever put into space.

2000 A crew begins living on board the International Space Station.

2001 The *Near Earth Asteroid Rendezvous (NEAR)* spacecraft becomes the first to land successfully on the surface of an asteroid when it lands on 433 Eros.

2003 The space shuttle *Columbia* explodes in flight, killing its seven-person crew.

2004 The Mars Exploration Rovers complete their mission on Mars.

Glossary

asteroid A rocky object orbiting the sun, mainly in a belt between Mars and Jupiter. The largest asteroid is around 620 miles (1,000 km) in diameter.

atmosphere The layers of gases that surround a planet or moon.

comet A small body in space made up of ice, snow, and grains of rock and dust.

communicate Send and receive messages to and from people or machines.

cosmonaut An astronaut from the former Soviet Union or present-day Russia.

galaxy A collection of many stars, planets, and gases held together by gravity.

gravity The pulling force between objects.

hydraulics A power system using liquids in cylinders, found in some space machines.

light-year A measure of distance in space. A light-year is the distance that light travels in one year—about 5.9 trillion miles (9.5 trillion km).

microgravity Very low gravity, as experienced by astronauts orbiting Earth.

NASA The National Aeronautics and Space Administration. This is the organization in charge of all space programs for the U.S.

orbit The path followed by an object in space as it goes around another object.

payload Important cargo that is carried on a space shuttle or a rocket.

planet A body in orbit around a star such as the sun.

radiation Energy that travels in waves.

satellite An object that orbits a planet or other body. Satellites can be natural, such as the moon, or man-made, such as communications satellites that relay TV pictures around Earth.

solar system The solar system is made up of the sun, the planets, their moons, asteroids, comets, and any other dust or gas in orbit around the sun.

star A massive, shining ball of very hot gas, such as the sun.

terraforming The process of altering the environment of a planet or moon to allow it to support life from Earth.

ultraviolet ray An invisible form of energy given off by the sun and other bodies in space.

Further Information

Further Reading

Angelo, Joseph A. *The Facts on File Space and Astronomy Handbook.* New York: Facts on File, 2002.

Gifford, Clive. *How to Live on Mars.* Oxford: Oxford University Press, 2001.

Stott, Carole. *DK Discoveries: Moon Landing.* New York: Dorling Kindersley, 1999.

Stott, Carole. *Eyewitness Guide: Space Exploration.* New York: Dorling Kindersley, 2002.

Web sites

http://kids.msfc.nasa.gov/Space/WhereTopics.asp
An up-to-date guide to where various rockets, satellites, and space stations are currently in orbit.

http://www.seti.org/
The Web site of the Search for Extraterrestrial Intelligence Institute. This organization researches life in space.

http://www.nasa.gov/audience/forstudents/5-8/features/index.html
A terrific collection of Web pages from NASA aimed at students interested in space and space exploration.

http://www.historychannel.com/exhibits/moonshots/main.html
A detailed timeline of space exploration provided by the History Channel.

http://www.esa.int/esaCP/index.html
The homepage of the European Space Agency. Read about their past, present, and future missions.

Index